"Paul's letter to the Ephesians has been one of the top five most influential New Testament books in the history of the church and Christian theology. It deserves to be read with care and prayer by each new generation. With the skill of a clear thinker and writer, Lynn Cohick explains the text succinctly, opens the letter up suggestively for those who are called to teach and preach the text, and—even more—leads us to adore the God of grace who brings together all people in Christ. This commentary will be long recommended for the parish pastor and Bible study teacher."

—SCOT McKNIGHT, Visiting Professor, Houston Theological Seminary

"Lynn Cohick brings together decades of research, writing, and teaching on Ephesians and makes it accessible to readers in this new volume in the *Proclamation* series. An ideal resource for pastors and students who want to understand Ephesians and its many complexities in a way that is comprehensible, useful, and even exciting."

—MICHAEL F. BIRD, Deputy Principal, Ridley College

"Utilizing her trademark skills as an exegete and historian, Cohick's clear prose and efficient comment make this commentary incredibly accessible and a delight to read. Even more, especially in the most complicated passages, Cohick's exacting insights brought multiple moments of clarity and deeper appreciation for this magisterial epistle. I will return to her insights in my study and in my classroom many times over."

—AMY PEELER, Professor of New Testament, Wheaton College

"Cohick, who has already published significant scholarship on Ephesians including an excellent technical commentary, lends her wisdom to preachers who aim to present this Pauline text as a compelling word for the people of God today. Her exegesis is trustworthy, her exposition is clarifying, and her homiletical counsel is practical and insightful."

—NIJAY K. GUPTA, Julius R. Mantey Professor of New Testament,
    Northern Seminary

"Biblical expertise expressed in clear and compelling language. Exegetical insights aimed at preaching and teaching. Scholarship for the church. These are the gifts that Lynn Cohick offers to preachers and teachers of Ephesians.

Her scholarly history with this Pauline letter and her love for the church mean that readers can rely on her wisdom. I highly recommend this book."

—JEANNINE K. BROWN, David Price Professor of Biblical and Theological Foundations, Bethel Seminary

"Already established as an expert commentator on Ephesians, in this volume Lynn Cohick brings her skills to the text for preaching and teaching. The result is a powerful, perceptive, and practical guide to the cosmic, saving work of the Triune God and its significance for the nitty-gritty of real life today. A gem of a book."

—MICHAEL GORMAN, Raymond E. Brown Professor of Biblical Studies and Theology, St. Mary's Seminary and University

Jan N. Bremmer and Marco Formisano, 103–17. Oxford: Oxford University Press, 2012.

Skinner, Matthew L. "Remember My Chains: New Testament Perspectives on Incarceration." *Interpretation* 72 (2018) 251–365.

Theocharous, Myrto. "The Image of God and Justice." In *John Stott: Living Radical Discipleship in All of Life*, edited by Laura S. Meitzner Yoder, 40–51. Carlisle, UK: Langham Global Library, 2021.

Thielman, Frank. *Ephesians*. BECNT. Grand Rapids: Baker Academic, 2010.

Thiselton, Anthony G. *The First Epistle to the Corinthians*. NIGTC. Grand Rapids: Eerdmans, 2000.

Thomson, D. P. *Eric H. Liddell: Athlete and Missionary*. Perth: Munro & Scott, 1971.

Thurston, Bonnie B., and Judith M. Ryan. *Philippians and Philemon*. Sacra Pagina. Collegeville, MN: Liturgical, 2004.

Toop, William. "Recollections of Eric Liddell by People Who Knew Him." http://www.ericliddell.org/eric-leddell/recollections/williamtoop.html.

Trebilco, Paul R. *The Early Christians in Ephesus from Paul to Ignatius*. Grand Rapids: Eerdmans, 2007.

Treier, Daniel J. *Lord Jesus Christ*. Grand Rapids: Zondervan Academic, 2023.

Walsh, Julie, and Jeffrey D. Miller. "Translating Ephesians 5.33." *Bible Translator* 74 (2023) 93–109.

Wassen, Cecilia. *Women in the Damascus Document*. Atlanta: Scholars, 2005.

Westfall, Cynthia Long. *Paul and Gender: Reclaiming the Apostle's Vision for Men and Women in Christ*. Grand Rapids: Baker Academic, 2016.

———. "'This Is a Great Metaphor!' Reciprocity in the Ephesians Household Code." In *Christian Origins and Greco-Roman Culture: Social and Literary Contexts for the New Testament*, edited by Stanley E. Porter and Andrew W. Pitts, 561–98. Leiden: Brill, 2013.

Yinger, K. L. "Interpretation: New Perspective." In *Dictionary of Paul and His Letters*, edited by Scot McKnight et al., 516–21. 2nd ed. Downers Grove, IL: IVP Academic, 2023.

www.ingramcontent.com/pod-product-compliance
Lightning Source LLC
Chambersburg PA
CBHW030308100426
42812CB00002B/618